Taxid

Copyright © 2013 Read Books Ltd.
This book is copyright and may not be
reproduced or copied in any way without
the express permission of the publisher in writing

British Library Cataloguing-in-Publication Data
A catalogue record for this book is available from the
British Library

Taxidermy

Taxidermy (from the Greek for *arrangement of skin*) is the art of preparing, stuffing, and mounting the skins of animals (especially vertebrates) for display (e.g. as hunting trophies) or for other sources of study. Taxidermy can be done on all vertebrate species of animals, including mammals, birds, fish, reptiles, and amphibians. A person who practices taxidermy is called a taxidermist. Taxidermists may practice professionally for museums or as businesses, catering to hunters and fishermen, or as amateurs, such as hobbyists, hunters, and fishermen. To practice taxidermy, one should be very familiar with anatomy, sculpture, and painting, as well as tanning.

The preservation of animal skins has been practiced for a long time. Embalmed animals have even been found with Egyptian mummies. Although embalming incorporates the use of lifelike poses, it is not technically considered taxidermy though. The earliest methods of preservation of birds for natural history cabinets were published in 1748 by the French Academician Réaumur, and four years later, techniques for mounting were described by M. B. Stollas. By the eighteenth century, almost every town had a tannery business. In the nineteenth century, hunters began bringing their trophies to upholstery shops, where the upholsterers would actually sew up the animal skins and stuff them with rags and cotton. The term 'stuffing' or a 'stuffed animal' evolved from this crude form of taxidermy. Professional taxidermists prefer the term 'mounting' to 'stuffing' however. More sophisticated cotton-wrapped wire bodies supporting sewn-on cured skins soon followed.

In France, Louis Dufresne, taxidermist at the *Muséum National d'Histoire Naturelle* from 1793, popularized arsenical soap (utilising the chemical Arsenic) in an article titled, *Nouveau Dictionnaire D'Histoire Naturelle* (1803–1804). This technique enabled the museum to build the greatest collection of birds in the world. Dufresne's methods spread to England in the early nineteenth century, where updated and non-toxic methods of preservation were developed by some of the leading naturalists of the day, including Rowland Ward and Montague Brown. Ward established one of the earliest taxidermy firms, Rowland Ward Ltd. of Piccadilly. Nevertheless, the art of taxidermy remained relatively undeveloped, and the specimens that were created remained stiff and unconvincing.

The golden age of taxidermy was during the Victorian era, when mounted animals became a popular part of interior design and decor. For the Great Exhibition of 1851 in London, John Hancock, widely considered the father of modern taxidermy, mounted a series of stuffed birds as an exhibit. They generated much interest among the public and scientists alike, who considered them superior to earlier models and were regarded as the first lifelike and artistic specimens on display. A judge remarked that Hancock's exhibit 'will go far towards raising the art of taxidermy to a level with other arts, which have hitherto held higher pretensions.'

In the early twentieth century, taxidermy was taken forward under the leadership of artists such as Carl Akeley, James L. Clark, Coleman Jonas, Fredrick and William Kaempfer, and Leon Pray. These and other taxidermists developed anatomically accurate figures which incorporated every detail in artistically interesting poses, with mounts in realistic settings and poses. This was quite a change from the caricatures popularly offered as hunting trophies. The methods of taxidermy have substantially improved over the last century, heightening quality and lowering toxicity. The animal is first skinned in a process similar to removing the skin from a chicken prior to cooking. This can be accomplished without opening the body cavity, so the taxidermist usually does not see internal organs or blood. Depending on the type of skin, preserving chemicals are applied or the skin is tanned. It is then either mounted on a mannequin made from wood, wool and wire, or a polyurethane form. Clay is used to install glass eyes, which are either bought or cast by the taxidermist themselves.

As an interesting side note, with the success of taxidermy has come the sub-genre of 'rogue taxidermy'; the creation of stuffed animals which do not have real, live counterparts. They can represent impossible hybrids such as the jackalope and the skvader, extinct species, mythical creatures such as dragons, griffins, unicorns or mermaids, or may be entirely of the maker's imagination. When the platypus was first discovered by Europeans in 1798, and a pelt and sketch were sent to the UK, some thought the animal to be a hoax. It was supposed that a taxidermist had sewn a duck's beak onto the body of a beaver-like animal. George Shaw, who produced the first description of the animal in the *Naturalist's Shunga Miscellany* in 1799, even took a pair of scissors to the dried skin to check for stitches. Today, although a niche craft, the art of taxidermy - rogue or otherwise, is still thriving.

CONTENTS

FORWARD

In the present day and age with wild game becoming increasingly scarce, bag limit and seasons greatly reduced, and some species fast disappearing from woods and field, it would seem that more information in the little known art of taxidermy should be made available.

The pleasure of many a trip afield can be increased a thousand-fold and perpetuated for many years to come by preserving some of the trophies by artistic mounting. It is to this end that the following pages are written.

No great skill is required in taxidermy and good comon sense and a degree of patience is all that is necessary to follow the easy, step by step methods of mounting small animals outlined in this manual.

The text and sketches should be studied thoroughly before making the initial start.

Have tools and materials laid out within easy reach of the work table and select a well lighted location. The tools and materials required are few and have been purposely selected for this work because they are easily obtainable in the average home and local community.

The methods described in this work apply to most of the common small mammals generally considered for mounting, up to the size of fox.

This booklet is not offered as a treatise on advanced taxidermy but rather as a guide for those with a naturalistic bent who would endeavor to do their own mounting without an elaborate outlay of funds for tools and materials.

Tools . . .

KNIFE—A good pocket or pen knife with a thin, keen blade.

SMALL WHETSTONE—for honing the knife blade.

SCRAPER—An old teaspoon or kitchen knife with one edge thinned makes a handy scraper for animal skins and bones.

NEEDLES—Taxidermists use curved, three-corner surgical needles, but large darning needles serve the purpose nicely. Set in the end of a small stick, they form a handy tool for adjusting eyelids, lips, etc.

FILE—For sharpening wires used in mounting.

OTHER—A small, pointed, cut-off nippers such as electricians use is a handy tool for cutting wire, bones, tough leg tendons, etc. A pair of shears will be found helpful as will other household tools such as pliers, saw, drill, etc. Most of these are readily available in the home. Stuffing rods, hooks, scrapers, etc. can easily be fashioned from pieces of wire hammered and filed to shape on one end, and a loop handle formed at the other.

Materials . . .

BORAX—Powdered borax may be purchased almost anywhere and is inexpensive. It is unparalled as a "preservative" and insect repellent and has largely replaced the old time arsenical poisoning of skins. Unlike arsenic, borax is absolutely safe to use and does not irritate the skin. Use borax by rubbing on all animal skins and bones. To make borax water wash for cleaning and soaking animal skins, sprinkle enough borax in warm water to make a saturated solution; that is, add enough that some remains undissolved on the bottom of the container, after stirring. Borax is also unexcelled for fluffing and drying animal skins that have been washed. Work the powder well into the fur or hair, than beat out with a small switch, when dry.

EXCELSIOR—Sometimes called wood wool. This material is widely used for packing fragile articles and is easily obtainable at drug and dept. stores where it can generally be had for the asking. Some of this material should be chopped into short lengths and can be mixed with cotton batting to be used as filling material. Retain some in its normal state for building up leg muscles, etc. in the larger mountings.

CLAY OR PAPIER MACHE—Papier mache, a commercially prepared product, comes in a dry form, and when mixed with water, produces the best medium for a multitude of purposes in taxidermy. However, because it is not available except through dealers in taxidermist supplies, the reader may substitute either potters clay or plastilene, (a form of modeling clay with an oil base) either of which may be purchased in most stores dealing in art supplies. In a pinch, even ordinary putty can be used.

COTTON BATTING—Upholsterers, furniture stores, etc. generally have this item on hand. Buy the coarse, shoddy type which works well and is inexpensive.

WIRE—Use only galvanized, annealed wire, obtainable at hardware stores. Size 10 to 16 (New standard guage) will cover most small animal jobs. Select a size just large enough to support the animal firmly. Remember too, that a mount stiffens up while drying, even though it seems a bit wobbly while in a "green" state.

SEWING THREAD—Ordinary carpet or machine thread, preferably of linen, is suitable for most small animal work. The local tailor usually has a variety of strong threads on hand or possibly the local dry goods store can supply it.

BEESWAX—A small piece is sufficient. Used to strengthen and waterproof the sewing thread.

COTTON CORD—On animals the size of coon, fox, etc., the muscles of the legs should be built up of cotton batting or excelsior which is wrapped firmly in place with cotton cord.

GLASS EYES—These are the only items which must be purchased by mail. Complete lines of American and imported glass eyes are carried by the majority of dealers in taxidermists supplies. (See Supplier list). It is advisable to have the correct artificial eyes for the animal being mounted on hand before the work is started. This poses a real problem, the only solution being to obtain a catalog before-hand and ordering a variety suitable for the specimens anticipated.

Mention the animal to the dealer for which eyes are desired and he will generally send the correct size and color.

The following comments may be of help in ordering a supply of glass eyes:

Most eyes are numbered according to their diameter in millimeters. Thus, a grey squirrel would take an eye approximately 12 MM or size 12. Solid black eyes are suitable for some of the rodents such as rats, mice and squirrels. They are also satisfactory for skunks, mink, otter and others of the weasel family. Raccoons take a black eye. Many animals take a brown eye with round black pupil. The cat family require a special eye, as do the foxes. Approximate sizes for a few of the common animals are:

Mouse	#3	Grey or Black	
Rat, Mole	#4	Squirrel, Porcupine	#12
Weasel	#6	Raccoon	#14
Red Squirrel	#9	Cottontail Rabbit	#15
Muskrat, Mink,		Fox	#16
Skunk, Fox, Squirrel,		Jack Rabbit	#17
Woodchuck, Opossum,	#11		

Step One- SKINNING

Before the skinning operation is started, it is well to jot down a few notes and sketches as to the physical proportions of the specimen. Take lineal measurements from point of nose to corner of eyes; point of nose to back of skull and point of nose to root of tail. Measure the length of tail from root to end of vertabrae (not to end of fur or hair).

Also, measurements of the circumference at chest and abdomen will be helpful. Outline sketches of limbs and head will be of great aid when final mounting is done.

Becoming familiar with the general contour of the animal in all the various natural attitudes is of the highest importance.

Lay the animal on its back, head to left, and proceed with the skinning as follows:

Make an incision with the knife starting at the base of the neck, down the center line to the vent. Be careful not to cut deeper than necessary to sever the skin, especially at the abdomen. Grasp the edges of the skin on each side of the incision between the thumb and fore-finger of each hand and pull the skin away from the body. With this start it should be an easy matter to pull the skin free with the fingers, around to the back of the animal until the body has been completely encircled, or nearly so. If the skin is too difficult to be freed from the body with the fingers alone, make use of the knife, cutting with careful, sweeping strokes against the skin. The amateur will soon get the knack of this cutting operation and before long will be wielding the knife swiftly and dexterously, making each stroke tell.

Work rearward from the abdomen until the junction points of the back legs are reached, then loosen the skin as far as possible around the thighs. By grasping the hind leg of the animal and bending the knee sharply upward, the skin can be made to slip over the knee joint. It is then possible to work the skin entirely free around the lower leg. Sever the skinned leg at the hip joint and complete the skinning of the leg by stripping down to the ankle. Repeat this operation with the other leg. If the animal is larger than a squirrel, retain the leg bones to the hip. Clean all flesh from the bones, but do not disjoint them. If the animal is the size of squirrel or smaller, the leg bones need not be retained, and the skinned legs are severed at the ankle joint.

Now free the skin from the back end of the body until the root of the tail is reached. If the animal has a thick fleshy tail, the skin should be split on its underside almost to its tip and tail bone removed. Most common animals have slender, bony tails such as that of the squirrel, fox, etc. and these need not be split, but are slipped off between the thumb and forefinger. If it is found too difficult to remove the tail bone with the fingers, clamp the root of the tail in a vise and with the help of two round sticks held in both hands, the most stubborn tail skins can be stripped.

The partly skinned animal will now appear as in sketch "A". Now impale the body on a strong wire hook and suspend from a rafter or other overhead point at a convenient working height. Pull the skin downward inverting it over the head as in peeling off a glove. Use the knife deftly, cutting on all sides as the skin is brought downward until the front legs halt the progress. These are encircled with the fingers until the skin is freed to the wrists in the same manner as the back legs. Here again retain the bones to the shoulder in the larger animals, but sever the entire leg at the wrist in animals the size of the squirrel or smaller.

When the skin has been drawn down to the skull, watch for the ear entrances. Extreme care must be taken here to cut close to the skull bone. Cut through the ear cartilage of the ear canal as close to the skull bone as possible.

After passing the ears, the eyes are reached and again extreme care must be taken to cut carefully, close to the bone. Stretch the skin over this point and cut forward until the transparent membrane covering the eye appears under the knife. One way to avoid mistakes is to place the finger tip against the eyeball from without and then cut against it until the entire eyelid is freed from the eyeball without cutting the delicate skin surrounding it.

Continue skinning down the front of the head to the nose, cutting the cartilage of the nose close to the bone and cutting the lips away from the skull at the gum line all around the mouth.

The skin is now completely freed from the body and will appear as in sketch "B".

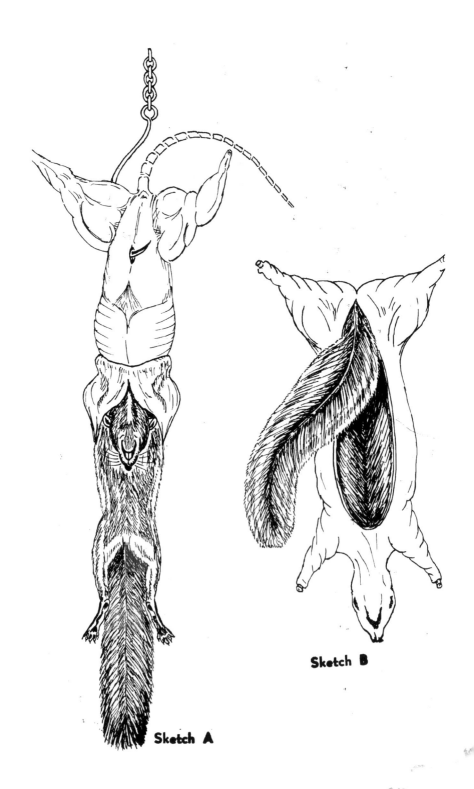

Sketch A

Sketch B

Step Two – PREPARING THE SKIN

Assuming that all the flesh has been scraped from the retained leg bones, attention must now be given to the paws or feet (of the larger animals). They should be incised on their undersides and as much flesh as possible removed from the foot and hand bones. After this is done, they may be rubbed thoroughly with powdered borax, packed to their original size with papier mache or clay and sewn up. Be sure to wax the sewing thread thoroughly.

Now go over the flesh side of the skin with the scraper, removing all evidences of adhering fat and bits of flesh. Some animals such as raccoon require more effort in this respect; in any event, time spent on this chore will be well repaid in the final mounting. Give special attention to the head portion of all skins. All adhering flesh must be shaved from areas around the eyes, nose and lips. Lips must be split to their edges and thinned out. The more lip skin retained the better, as this allows better control of mouth details later. With extreme care, and judicious use of the knife, the nostril linings can be freed from their cartilaginous fastenings and the entire nose thinned to a flexible condition. This provides for easier nose modeling later and will prevent the unnatural, wrinkled appearance apparent in many poorly mounted specimens.

Ears, too, must receive attention, the butts cleansed of excess cartilage and all flesh removed. Where possible, and this is important, ears should be skinned to their tips on all animals larger than squirrel. This is generally an easy proposition. The skin on the back of the ears is separated from the cartilage lining and the entire ear is inverted. A small, flat, hardwood paddle may be of help, but most taxidermists use only the fingers. Of course, care must be taken to avoid tearing the thin ear skins.

Now clean the fur side of the animal, removing any blood stains, grease spots, etc. with a weak solution of ammonia water. Warm soapy water with a little borax added is a good cleanser for very dirty skins and even soaking the entire skin in a saturated borax water solution is recommended. In fact, such soaking, together with subsequent fluffing of furs with dry powdered borax pays dividends later because a skin thus handled will be practically moth proof throughout its life.

Rub borax in thoroughly, on all parts of the skin, on bones, ears, nostrils, etc.

At this time, prepare a set of ear liners cut to fit the ear skins perfectly. Use light weight fiber or high grade cardboard for this purpose. These should be dipped in hot wax or painted with shellac for waterproofing. Thin sheet lead, if available, may also be used if the ears are large. Be sure to insert the ear liners before placing the artificial skull in the head skin. They may be held in place with a stitch or two with needle and thread, the stitches being removed after drying.

When all this has been accomplished, the skin is ready for wiring and final mounting.

Step Three- *THE ARTIFICIAL SKULL*

There are a number of methods of preparing the artificial skull, several of which will be discussed here.

Sever the skull from the neck, close to the base of the bony structure and lay it on a sheet of paper and, with a pencil held vertically, trace its outline as seen from above. Then hold it on its side and trace its contours as viewed from the side. Indicate on the sketch, the location of eyes, jaws, teeth, etc. and make an accurate picture for use in preparing the artificial skull.

Some taxidermists use the original bony structure of the skull, rebuilding muscles and tissue removed by the use of papier mache or clay, while others prefer a hand carved wooden facsimile. Still another method is to make a plaster cast of the original skull and use it as a mold to prepare a skull made of layers of compressed paper. However, the latter method is beyond the scope of this article and it is easier and more practical to use either of the first two methods outlined.

It is suggested that if the animal being mounted is the size of squirrel or smaller, the amateur proceed as follows: Clean the original skull thoroughly, removing all meat and tissue, eyeballs, tongue, and brain. Remove the brain with a small wire hook through the occipital opening at the base of the skull. This work can be facilitated by parboiling the skull in water.

When the skull is thoroughly cleaned, rub it well with borax. Now, replace the muscles and tissue removed by building up with modeling clay or papier mache. Round off the skull until it resembles the sketches made earlier. It can now be laid aside while proceeding with the next operation.

If the animal being mounted is larger than a squirrel, it is recommended that an artificial skull be carved as close to the contours of the original as possible from a block of some soft wood such as white pine or balsa. Balsa wood has the advantage of being light and is easy to handle. With the aid of sharp knives and wood rasps, this carving need not be difficult.

Be particularly careful when carving the lips; undercutting the upper lip and forming a groove or lip pocket around the entire mouth into which the lip skin may be tucked and pinned.

Sand the carving when finished and give it a coat of clear shellac.

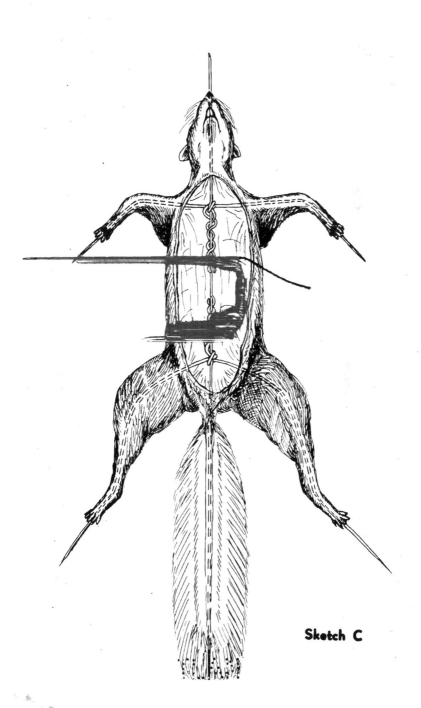

Sketch C

Sketch D

Step Four- WIRING ASSEMBLY

In Step One it was explained that it was unnecessary to retain leg bones of the smaller animals. Assuming that the work is being done on such an animal, proceed as follows: Cut two pieces of wire of correct weight and two and one half times the length of one front leg from foot to shoulder joint. Cut two more pieces two and one half times the length of one back leg from foot to hip joint. These are the leg wires and each should be sharpened at one end to a smooth tapering point.

Now cut another piece of the same wire one and one half times the length of body, from tip of nose to root of tail. This will be the body wire and is also sharpened at one end. Cut a sixth wire one and one half times the length of tail and sharpen it.

Stretch the prepared skin fur side out on the work table and insert the prepared skull into the head skin. Take the sharpened end of the body wire and force the point through the base of the skull (slightly above the occipital opening) and push through the skull until it emerges at the nasal cavity. Let the end of the wire pass through one of the nostrils of the skin for several inches. Now, at a point where the shoulders begin, whip the body wire into a small loop. See sketch "C" Make this loop just large enough to admit two of the leg wires. Then, at a point just forward of the hip line, turn a similar loop in the body wire. Clinch the wire to itself with a turn or two, then cut off the remainder, if any. See sketch "C". Now insert one of the foreleg wires into the bottom of the foot and force it through the foot until it appears within the skin. Pull it through the upper loop of the body wire a short distance. Repeat this wiring operation on the other leg. Then twist the ends of the two leg wires tightly to the body wire as shown in sketch "C".

The tail wire is the next consideration. Spin a quantity of cotton batting on it, wrapped smoothly in place with cord. Refer to measurements and sketches. Make sure the artificial tail is just *slightly* smaller than the original, tapering it evenly toward its sharpened end. Wet the artificial tail with water, then rub well with borax. Now insert it into the tail skin until the sharpened end is forced through the tip. Feed the butt end of the tail wire through the lower body wire loop and wrap the excess around the body wire. Now wire the rear legs in the same fashion as the front, crossing them through the rear loop and twisting both tightly to the body wire.

In mounting animals larger than squirrel (those in which leg bones were retained), the wiring is accomplished in much the same manner except that the leg muscles are built up of cotton batting during the wiring operation. (See sketch "D"). When the leg wire has been brought through the foot to a point just beyond the upper leg bone, bind the bones loosely to the wire at several places. Then build up the artificial muscular structure of the leg by wrapping with cotton batting, bound with turns of cord around the bone-wire assembly. Refer to sketches made earlier to get these properly shaped. When the leg has been smoothly built up to the proper contours, the leg wire is pulled through the body wire loops and twisted thereon as explained above.

Step Five- FINAL MOUNTING

Again assuming that the animal being mounted is of the smaller type, proceed with the final mounting as follows: Take small wads of cotton batting and tamp them lightly in the neck skin close to the skull. Be sure to pack the cotton evenly on all sides of the body wire, as it is important that this wire remain centered in the mount and that it does not come to the surface under the skin where it would show. Continue filling the neck skin as evenly as possible until it is filled to the shoulders. Then with the aid of a small stuffing rod, made from a piece of scrap wire, stuff the front leg skins using small wads of the batting at first, where the lower parts are thin and narrow, and increasing the size where the legs widen out. It is important that this stuffing be done in a careful efficient manner, using just the right amount of filling, evenly packed around the leg wire. Avoid getting a lumpy effect by pushing the filling around within and by squeezing from the outside with the fingers. The legs may be stuffed rather tightly *but be careful not to overstuff. In fact, overstuffing is probably the greatest mistake made by most amateurs.*

When the fore quarters have been filled satisfactorily, do the same with the rear legs using the same procedure. Now start sewing up the incision with needle and well-waxed thread. Take a few stitches loosely, then pick out any fur or hair that may be caught, and draw up snugly. The best stitch to use is that in which the point of needle is always inserted from the under, or flesh side, i.e. from inside out. Sew the incision part way down, starting at the head end. Then continue the stuffing operation, packing the body skin evenly on all sides. Remember to keep the body wire well centered and equally surrounded on all sides with the packing. A good way to avoid the body wire from working through the packing when the mount is posed later, is to lay a broad strip of batting directly under the body wire throughout its entire length.

Continue sewing and stuffing alternately until the task is completed.

This stuffing operation is done in exactly the same way in the larger animals except, of course, that only the body skin need be filled, the legs having been taken care of previously.

When the stuffing operation has been completed, pose the animal in the desired attitude. Here is where natural aptitude shows up, for the real test in mounting skill, lies in the ability of the taxidermist to mold his work into a re-creation of the natural form. Fasten the mount to a temporary base board drilled to receive the leg wires. Go over the body carefully with the fingers, smoothing out any irregularities, lumps and hollows that should be corrected. With the thumb and forefinger many of these defects can be adjusted by pressing and squeezing. If there are hollows that cannot be corrected by pressure on either side, take a sharp awl or upholsterer's regulator, forcing the point through the skin and picking the filling underneath until it fills out the depression.

Now give attention to the head. Adjust the head skin carefully on the skull, paying particular attention to ears and eyes. Fill out the eye openings with clay and insert the glass eyes, adjusting the lids with a needle until an expression of alive interest is secured. Be sure the eyes are set at the correct depth, protruding slightly but not having a bulgy appearance.

Insert a small quantity of clay or mache into the ear butts from the outside and press the ears into shape with the fingers. A pin or two in the correct spots will help hold the ears in place.

Finally, adjust the nose and mouth details. A little clay or mache strategically placed in the nostrils facilitates the smooth modeling of this important point. Fill a little material in the lips if necessary, adjusting the lower lip first. If a wooden skull was used and a lip groove provided as was suggested, the work is much simplified. Tuck the lip skin into the groove evenly, around its entire length. Secure the lips with common straight pins, using as many as necessary to hold them in place. A few well placed stitches with needle and thread in the mouths of small rodents such as muskrats, squirrels, etc. will hold the lips in place in cases where exposed teeth are desired.

The mount may now be put away in a dry, airy place to dry. Check the specimen occasionally while it is drying and correct any distortion about the face which may occur.

When the mount is completely dry, it may be removed from its temporary base and secured on a permanent one. Remove pins and cut the excess wire protruding from skull and tail. Comb the fur and apply color to claws, nose, lips and eyelids where necessary.

It is suggested that many of our native game animals be mounted on wall panels in various natural attitudes perhaps with rustic or hand painted backgrounds. These panels are hung on the wall and as such are usually beyond the reach of curious admirers who have a habit of handling mountings which shouldn't be handled.

Try to be original in the work. The possibilities are unlimited to those who put their imagination to use, with an eye to something attractive and different.

24900612R00016

Printed in Great Britain
by Amazon